Food For You:

Buying it cheap, using each piece, and finding it free.

Dody Mitchell

ISBN-13: 978-1493666812

ISBN-10: 1493666819

Dedicated to:

My beautiful daughters four, of whom my whole being adores.

Prologue

When we start this journey in life, we never end up where we expect. Growing up, I had very little instruction in anything related to taking care of a family. I had always hoped that someone would teach me. On occasion, I came across some family member or foster parent that would, but these instances were too brief and too few to glean a true appreciation for the domestic arts.

It has fallen out of favor to steward one's resources well. It is seen as being miserly or worse. People like to believe that they have found a way out of the chains of reality. When I try to explain to people that working more does not necessarily translate into a better life, they scoff at me. I have had people ridicule my manner for training up my children as rearing "princes" and "princesses" of poverty. I want to know, when did our nation scoff at the idea of industry inside the home as being economically viable?

There are few things more valuable than knowing how to buy the cheapest healthy food, using that food to its last crumb without waste, and finding food free. This is somewhat of an art form. In order to do well, one must have taken the time to study the matter, employ all of their available resources, and utilize several methods. Most people don't even attempt this. This is for those that are willing to accept that home industry employed in stewarding one's own resources is just as valuable as industry outside of the home employed in utilizing someone else's resources to procure more money for them. It is for those ladies or gentlemen that have had little training in the domestic arts and find themselves in great need of that training suddenly.

Even so, those of you that have had a great deal of experience may find a tid bit or two. I only hope that I can satisfy you with my wit and banter if you are more experienced than I. I have been a mother to six with next to nothing for income for some time. That is why I feel I am qualified to write this book. If I can provide for six on so little, imagine what you can do with your own income.

Table of Contents

Introduction.

Food For You is meant to be a beginners guide to buying healthy food cheap, using all of that food up so that none is wasted, and to finding the occasional free food. It does not address organic foods, growing food, GMO foods, foods from the sea, or any other food related issues outside of price and variety. With that said, our own family does not eat seafood or cows. We avoid any foods grown on the west coast of the United States, in Japan, and in China due to the Fukishima nuclear plant disaster. This is our family, you may not feel it is important to avoid. We also avoid GMO's when we know they are present in foods. It is very difficult to do so as they are not labeled at the time of this writing in the United States. Where you live, it may be easier to find labeled foods.

GMO's are banned from being distributed in Algeria. Venezuela, Ecuador, Bulgaria, New Zealand, and Peru, has banned the cultivation of GMO seeds for commercial purposes. If you keep this in mind when shopping, it may help to alleviate some of the confusion.

Chapter One: Health First

Food is the very stuff that you are made of. Your body was built with food and clean water. It is maintained with food and clean water. It is one of the most important resources we require to live every single day. That is why it is so very important to choose the best food for our health. Everyone's health is different and due to that, everyone needs a different diet. There are some things that are universal to all people though when it comes to diet.

Non-processed foods are always best. Non-processed foods contain less chemicals, they are fresher, and they are generally cheaper per pound or kilogram. Non-processed foods would be fresh apples, rice, chicken legs, a head of cabbage, or cherries. Non-processed foods may have been altered slightly, after all chickens are slaughtered and butchered for market. They are foods that are in a state that may decay. That means, they are not grossly manipulated until they are unrecognizable to our ancestors. Rice is generally good for 6 months, so it is a slow decaying food. It is a very good staple food. It is inexpensive. Its great right, but you can't live on it alone. It is considered a whole food and a non-processed food.

Eating whole, non-processed foods whenever possible will save you money and save your health. Processed foods are full of sodium, preservatives, and empty calories. They are high in carbohydrates, low on fiber, and all around bad for you. There are some exceptions to this rule, but mostly, avoid as much of it as you can while keeping your budget under control.

Feel free to amend any suggestions as needed for your personal health needs. If you are diabetic, you might need to focus on lower carb meals. If you have Crohns, you may need to reduce your bean intake. Now, let's get reacquainted with food.

A staple food is something that is inexpensive, plentiful, somewhat healthy in moderate amounts, and usually easy to store for longer periods. Some examples of staple foods are corn, oats, barley, buckwheat, rye, spelt, amaranth, flax, wheat, rice, beans, potatoes, quinoa, etc. A staple food is necessary. In America, most people consider wheat, corn, soybeans, and rice staple foods. For our purposes, we will only deal in those items we can see at our local grocery store as a whole food. If we buy the food whole, we know that it is that food.

Staple foods are easy to find all over. You can find them in Kroger, Walmart, Target, Aldi, and various independent grocers. Staple foods can be found online at specialty stores like Bob's Red Mill or buy anything stores like Amazon. There is even humorous websites that supply serious food like Round Eye Supply.

Staple foods are not enough to keep us healthy and happy. Eating a full pound of potatoes may fill you, but you'll also feel pretty sick after. Vegetables are the next component of an inexpensive meal that is required for good health. Vegetables supply our vitamins and fiber. Without vegetables, our food is not as healthy or filling. They help to keep cravings in check.

Vegetables are found at local grocery stores, at farmer's markets, at local community supported agriculture, at neighborhood gardens, at roadside stands, and in our own gardens. Vegetables are what bulks up our inexpensive meals and gives it the flavor.

Finally, protein is the last component to a healthy meal. There are many varieties of protein including beans, which are considered a staple food. For our purposes here, we will focus on protein that supplies the body with bioavailable B 12. Protein that supplies the body with this B 12 is only found in animal sources. This would include milk, eggs, cheese, and animal flesh. Obviously, this diet is not vegan friendly. Modify, as you deem necessary.

Cooking aids that are necessary for a healthy diet would be oils and fats. Our protein will more than likely have some fat in it, but we also require some other fats in our diet. Some fats that are used for cooking and are healthy include; olive oil, grape seed oil, walnut oil, sesame oil, sunflower oil, butter, and ghee. Fats carry the flavor to our tongues. They are essential to making a person feel psychologically satisfied. Which fats you cook with will be determined by what you plan to cook. Finally, never choose margarine. Margarine is the cheapest "fat" on the market for cooking, but it is very bad for your body.

Wait you say, I forgot fruits. Fruit is a wonderful addition to any meal. However, fruit is not absolutely essential to survival. Fruit does contain vitamin C, but so do vegetables. Peppers, Brussels sprouts, broccoli, tomato, spinach, parsley, kale, leeks, and even potato skins all have vitamin C. Fruit should be considered a dessert after a nice meal. Fruit is not essential, but very nice to finish off with something sweet.

Chapter Two: Required Equipment

In order to make use of the food you intend to buy you will need a minimum amount of equipment. Where you buy or find the equipment is up to you. If you find you need a piece of equipment, try to find it second hand as this is cheaper. Also, keep in mind the size of your family when purchasing items. You will want something that can make at least two meals. Every time you cook, you will be cooking enough for two or more meals to put back for later.

Freezer: The very first thing you need to implement this frugal way of buying, cooking, and eating, is a freezer. Without it, you are limited to only buying the cheapest foods and hoping you use them up well. It also regulates you to cooking a full meal every time you want to eat from whole foods. This is not the easiest time efficient means of providing your daily meals. Tiny chest freezers of 5 cubic feet can be found for only $140-$190 brand new and suffice for a single person, a young couple, or even a young couple with a toddler. My own 5 cubic foot freezer was in service for a family of five before it just became too tiny to be of use and we had to buy an additional freezer. These freezers can fit in a corner in your apartment. In fact, when I first got mine I lived in a tiny apartment in Connecticut. I know a freezer seems like a huge appliance, but a small chest freezer is doable in a small apartment.

Crock-Pot: A crock-pot is a life saving device for the mom or dad that cannot stay up all night cooking. Okay, I exaggerated a little bit. These electrical pots heat food for you while you are out or sleeping. Alternatively, solar ovens will heat food for you while you are out also. If you want something truly unique, that uses no energy that you pay for, and have plenty of sunshine, a solar oven may be better than a crock-pot. Research both choices before purchasing. From experience, a solar oven is not as reliable as a crock-pot is in the extreme northern or southern latitudes and they are very hard to find second hand. I have both a crock-pot and a solar oven. I use the crock-pot all year and the solar oven on bright sunny summer days.

Stove or Oven: Not everything can be cooked in a crock-pot. You will need a little camp stove, a wood stove, a solar oven, hot plate, electric skillet, or something other than just a crock-pot. Preferably something, that has both a range and an oven. Notice that I did not suggest a microwave oven.

Microwaves have their place, but for cooking full meals, it should just be left alone. This book will assume that you own both a stove and an oven. You can modify recipes to cook in your device if you are limited to one.

Cookie Sheet: One cookie sheet for each rack in your oven is all that is required for most families. Most ovens have two racks. If you have a very large oven and a smaller than average cookie sheet set, you could fit two cookie sheets per rack. Try it out, if you can get as much as your oven can hold. My wood stove has three places to place cookie sheets in it. Cookie sheets are used for cookies, but you can also cook many other things on them. I have cooked vegetables, chicken legs, pork chops, potatoes, homemade French fries, turkey burgers, sausage, and much more on my cookie sheets.

Metal Spatula: A metal spatula is used to remove items from cookie sheets, hot frying pans, and grills. Metal spatulas are flat and can wedge themselves under food that is sticking to a pan.

Frying Pan or Wok: A frying pan is ok, but if you have an oven, they are not necessary. If you have an oven and a range, buy a wok instead. You can cook scrambled eggs in it all the same, but you can also cook stir-fry in it. Woks are the one pot wonder meal makers like a crock-pot. The differences being these are used on a range top like a frying pan. My wok sits down in the flames on my wood stove. This gets the bottom and the sides of the wok hot. In the summer, we use a little propane camp stove with our wok and it works just fine then too.

Pot: Two pots are the minimum for a good working kitchen. You need one pot that is large and one that is a small saucepot. I have one 12-quart pot and one 1-quart pot. These two pots have been with me for over ten years and have served me just fine. Avoid any pots with a non-stick coating if possible. Also, avoid any pots with plastic on them. If your pots have no plastic handles, you can use them as cake pans to bake in the oven with. They can also be used as roasting pans for small chickens and small hams. My 12-quart pot is great for that. If you want to be able to use it for both purposes, you can remove the handles. Just be sure to be extra careful when handling them.

Lids: Your pots and frying pan or wok should all have snug fitting lids. Lids are required for some dishes. For cooking rice, your big pot will absolutely need a lid. If you bought your equipment used, it may not have a lid. If so look for lids at your local discount stores, or from the second hand shops.

Oven Mittens: One pair of good oven mittens will save you a lifetime worth of burn blisters. In addition, quite a few scars and doctor visits. They are an absolute must. They are safety equipment meant to keep our fingers safe from high heat. They are used for all situations where high heat may burn us. You can use them to take a hot pot off the stove range or out of the oven.

Roasting Pan: If you plan on making a large turkey, goose, ham, leg of lamb, rack of ribs, or anything large, you will need a roasting pan. Roasting pans double as cake pans too, so they're not a waste of your money to own.

Spoon: One large metal spoon, one metal slotted spoon, and one wooden spoon are all the spoons you should need to cook.

Rubber Spatula: A rubber spatula comes in handy when baking. I have one made of silicone that stays good even in 500 degree Fahrenheit or 260 degree Celsius heat. I paid a dollar for it new. You can probably find one used for half that if it is a worry. They are very useful.

Large Bowl: A large bowl is very handy for serving salad greens plucked from the garden, to mixing up a batch of homemade bread. You only need one large bowl. My family has 8 people in it. If we can live with one large bowl, so can you. The good news is, if you take care of it, it will last a lifetime.

Colander, Juicer, or Steamer Basket: A colander or steamer basket can be used for the same things. I prefer a steam basket as it is better made. I'm not talking about the one dollar hanging baskets which look like chain links. I am talking about a juicer basket that doubles as a steamer basket, and triples as a colander. It's stainless steel, 3 parts, and always in use. It can also be used to extract essential oils out of herbs. In a pinch, they can be used to distill water. A steamer/juicer is worth its weight in gold. They can be purchased off amazon for $50 to $150 new. I have seen them sell for $10 used. They are stainless steel, have tubing which extracts off the juice, this juice can be further refined to remove essential oils, the basket works as a steamer, and the bottom a water pot.

Masher: This hand held utensil has one wire coming out of the handle that waves back and forth before going back into the handle. This creates mashed potatoes, smoothies, refried beans and much more with a little muscle. It is about a dollar new at most places and 25 to 50 cents used. It makes no difference if you buy them used or new.

Tongs: My kids get a kick out these things every time I say their name. For some reason they always think of thongs, like the underwear. A nice pair of metal tongs can pluck ears of corn out of a boiling bath, pull meat off a hot grill, pull hot pots closer so they can be retrieved from the oven, hold the drumstick of a turkey still while cutting, and more. They are my extended hands. Get good ones as the cheaper ones will always fail when you are holding something hot.

Carving Fork: A nice two-prong carving fork is about a dollar new and so nice to use when carving up a nice baked chicken. It is not an absolute *must* have, but it saves a lot of pain. You can find these used for 25 to 50 cents. I have had people give me theirs because they used it so infrequently. I found out they only used it infrequently because they ate a lot of processed foods.

Measuring Cups: These are vital for finding the exact amount needed for recipes. They can be found new for a dollar in local retail shops or for half of that used at thrift stores. At yard sales, they can be found for a quarter to fifty cents. You should have 1 cup, 1/2 cup, 1/3 cup, 1/4 cup, and 1/8 cup or else it is not a complete set. If it does not have all of these sizes, you can haggle them down to half the asking price. If they swear it "came that way," say you really need all of those sizes and stick to your guns.

Measuring Spoons: Again, these are vital for measuring the quantity of foodstuffs that are meant to be used in recipes. Measuring spoons can be found for a dollar in retail shops, fifty cents to as low as a quarter in thrift shops, and yard sales anywhere from fifty cents to ten cents. A proper spoon set will have a Tbsp., which means one Table Spoon, a tsp. that means 1 teaspoon, 1/2 teaspoon, 1/3 teaspoon, 1/4 teaspoon, and 1/8 teaspoon. If the set does not have all of these sizes, haggle down by half. Sometimes they will just give them to you.

Ice Cream Scoop: Why an ice cream scoop? Well, they are very useful for keeping your portion sizes in check. All ice cream scoops hold two to four ounces of food. If you buy a 2 to 3 ounce ice cream scoop, a person could easily keep track of their diet. One scoop of cooked rice is about a serving. Two scoops of vegetables are about a serving. One scoop of protein is about a serving. Of course, this is just a guesstimate. It varies per person. However, it is an easier way to keep track of food intake than measuring everything to the exact amount. It also helps meal planning and storage.

Chapter Three: Price Book and Expenditure Book

The first key to buying things cheaply, is to know where the cheapest price is at the moment. The second key is to know when things will be their cheapest before they are. There are several ways to go about this, but a good old fashion price book is a must for local mom and pop stores that are not integrated completely with the internet.

Setting up your price book should be easy. A page should look like this. On the top, you state what you are buying, for example a 12-ounce tin can of diced tomatoes. Along the left side, you place the brand names of 12-ounce cans of tinned tomatoes you intend to buy. Along the top, you would have the stores you have price checked. Inside this is the information. On the right hand side, you would place the date that information was collected. It is a spreadsheet. Another method is to place the upc code on the left hand side and to record the unit price under the store name. You could print it out, three hole punch it, place in a binder and fill it out as you go shopping.

Perhaps that's a little too old fashion for you, so you could take your tablet to the store and type in prices as you go. Before you go to the store, price check the items online and plug those numbers in your spreadsheet. Pre-plugging the information into your spreadsheet will save time looking it up at Amazon.com while you shop. That way you can see at a glance if it is cheaper online and have fewer distractions while you shop.

As you shop, write down all the prices you need and circle in red pen the one you bought that day. This helps to keep track of what you bought that day. This in the long term helps you to keep track of expenses.

If you are having trouble plugging in your information from online sources, there are several free apps to help with that. One such app is Price check by Amazon that is free for iphone and Android users. You "buy" the android app free off Amazon.com. If you have an iphone, you can download it off itunes free. You simply scan the items bar code or take a picture of it to get the price.

Another good free app to help comparison shop is Pic2Shop. It works on iphones, Android, and Windows phones. You just scan the bar code and then it comparison shops for you based on your location.

A price book is still a must because, it isn't just good for comparison shopping with the internet, it is best for comparison shopping with other local retail outlets and keeping a record of what prices were at a particular time. No apps above record how much prices were over a long period of time. They also don't keep track of when or where you bought your goods.

In order to get the maximum return on your price book, you will need to fill it out for at least a year. I personally have this as an "ongoing" project. It helps to see where price spikes are as well. I can get Chicken Ramen from Wal-Mart for about $4 a 12 pack. Amazon wants to charge $12 for two 12 packs of Chicken Ramen with free shipping. Obviously, Wal-Mart is cheaper even with free shipping in this case. However, I wouldn't know about the "super sale" Amazon is having on two 12 packs of spicy Cajun Ramen for $5 with free shipping if I were using an app in the store since Wal-Mart doesn't carry it. I would only know this by looking it up ahead of time on Amazon and putting that information into my spreadsheet.

A price book takes time to maintain. It isn't as fashionable to run around with a big bulky binder or even a tablet getting all the information into your spreadsheet. It might even be socially embarrassing for some people. It's important though to make sure you are not getting ripped off. The retailer's job is only to sell you what they say they are going to sell you for the *highest* price you will pay. Remember that.

Another thing I like to do is to keep a secondary book of expenditures. This I do mainly online using receipts. I keep a second temporary one in the house for about a month while I work on putting it all online.

This is really simple. It's very basic accounting, without all the confusing terms. We will be using basic cash accounting methods since it is best for seeing how much of a reserve you have.

It's done on a spread sheet. On the top, you would put the month and the previous month's total. Then on the top line of boxes you would put, Item Description, Income, Expenditure, Total, and Date. Incomes are positive numbers and expenditures are negative numbers. After each entry, add the latest entry to the previous total to find the new total. You should record any income or expenditures immediately into your spreadsheet. It makes it easier to keep track of what you still have left in reserve.

At the end of each month, take the final total and place it on the line that says previous month's totals for your new spreadsheet. It should also be your starting total for the next month.

This method of accounting is allowed for small businesses that make fewer than 5 million dollars a year and that do not hold a large amount of inventory. However, we will be using it for our household budget. One of the oversights of this method of accounting is debt. If you have large amounts of debt, it doesn't show you how much you owe in total. This is easy to keep track of on the household level, but not on the business level. Any good small business will computer their books using the cash basis and the accrual basis of accounting if they want to know how much they have in reserve and how much they owe. I digress, that is for another book.

To keep track of your debts, keep a secondary page in your expenditure book for each month. At the top place the month and the previous months total debt. On the top line write owed to, debt, payments, remaining balance, interest rate with how often applied, total debt owed, and date. This will help to keep track of how much you owe in aggregate, who you owe the most, and who is going to be getting the most interest out of you. The best idea is to pay off the highest balances first. Usually this is credit card debt. Then snow ball the debt you owe towards paying off those things you owe the least on.

Chapter Four: Stock up on Sales

After you have your price book set up and a good track record of what price happens when and where, you are ready to take advantage of sales. Let's explain how this goes. Every November toward the end of the month, my local small town grocer very close to my home has insane sales on Thanksgiving fixings. Turkeys are 69 cents a pound. Sweet potatoes are 29 cents a pound at this time. Butter goes down to 2 dollars a pound. Powdered and sweeten condensed milk drop in price almost 30%. Canned pumpkin is 69 cents a can. Cranberries, which can be kept in the freezer, drop to a dollar fifty a pound. For the rest of the year the prices on these items are never this low.

I only know that they are the cheapest they will ever be and the cheapest anywhere because of my price book. Since so many things go to rock bottom prices this month where I live, I save as much money as I can to stock up on food during this month. Since I have a lot of spare freezer space, I buy two to four turkeys. I would buy enough stuffing for two to three months. I buy enough sweet potatoes that I will have plenty through Christmas. I buy enough canned pumpkin to make one pie a month for the whole year. The same thing goes for condensed sweetened milk.

The biggest "saver" on this list is the turkey. Once turkey meat goes below 69 cents a pound, I try to buy a year's supply of turkey to freeze. I do this because I know that meat through the entire year never drops below 69 cents a pound in my area. That is not hamburger, not chicken legs on sale, not fish on manager specials; nothing drops below 69 cents a pound.

The price book is very handy for showing where the lowest price point has been for an item throughout the year, but it can also show the lowest price point an entire group of foods has been at, when it was the lowest, and which item it was in that group. Once you find the lowest staple and lowest protein, you can stock up for the year. Vegetables are harder to stock up on for a year. However, I would still purchase a lot of whatever vegetable was at the lowest price and the lowest for the year, to freeze.

For a family of eight to get enough protein for the whole year from whole turkeys, it takes a lot of freezer space. To get around this obstacle, the turkeys are roasted as soon as we get home, take the meat off the carcass, and freeze it in ½ to 1 pound sizes inside of Ziploc bags. Working in this way, almost a years' worth of protein can be frozen and laid aside for later.

Not everything you buy will belong in the freezer. Canned goods can be kept on shelves, in plastic tote boxes, under beds, in a pantry, in the closet on the floor, under a dresser, under an entertainment center, just about anywhere there is room. Canned goods last for almost a year after their expiration date. If any cans are puffy, dented, or spurt when opened, throw the can away because it may have been contaminated.

If you are storing staples, you can take several methods depending on the size of your household. For small households, you can save empty food jars from pasta sauce, peanut butter, tin coffee cans, and the like to reuse. You just wash the container very well and dry it very well. After it is 100% dry, you can partition out dry beans, rice, spelt, wheat kernels, dried corn, amaranth seeds, quinoa, and more into these containers from bulk bags and boxes. Oxygen absorbers or moisture absorbers will prolong their shelf life. Then the containers can be stored where canned goods are stored. Dried staple foods will keep for 6 months or longer.

For a large family to store dry staples it requires a little more work that is creative. Families of five or more should consider investing into FDA food safe square buckets. These can be found at Uline and many other business-to-business stores. I would suggest at least two buckets for rice and two bucket for beans.

Our house has two rice buckets, two bean buckets, one sugar bucket, and one oatmeal bucket. 2 Tablespoons of food grade diatomaceous earth will keep bugs out of your grains and beans. Food grade diatomaceous earth can be found online. It is safe for consumption in these low quantities and helps to rid cats and dogs of intestinal worms. If moisture absorbers are added also, the staple goods will last longer. Just be careful to pick them out of anything you intend to cook before you do cook it.

When you store a lot of food, you need a system for keeping track of it. One old fashioned way is to put the item and total number bought down on a piece of paper. Then as you use each thing simply make a mark next to the item to signify one is gone. When the marks total almost as much as the amount that was in storage, it's time to buy more.

A much more modern way is the free My Pantry App, which not only keeps track of your pantry, but shopping lists coupons and more. It only works on Android phones. My Pantry 2.0 is also great, but it costs money. You can find them both at Google Play.

For iphone there is the free app Inventory Scanner an app that can handle the pantry inventory or a small business. This app can handle at least 12 different types of bar codes, making your job as easy as pointing and scanning.

Chapter Five: Coupons

Everyone knows that coupons can save you money, but I have met very few people that know how to use coupons to their fullest potential. Coupons are the ever-elusive holy grail of cutting your grocery bill according to many, but I disagree. Coupons help, but they do not work alone unless you are a master at couponing. Luckily, with the resources provided, you will become a master at using coupons in no time.

First, you have to find coupons. They can be found in local papers. You can get your local paper for less if you go through Discountednewspapers.com. You can also just buy the inserts themselves, uncut, from Sunday Coupon Inserts, Saving my Family Money, and Shop Whole Coupon Inserts.

You can also hire someone to cut coupons out for you, for a nominal fee of 8 cents or 12 cents each. The Coupon Clippers and Klip2Save.com are two sites that I have used with great satisfaction for this service. At the TheCouponClippers.com you can download and print free coupons too.

Other places you can print coupons are at Coupons.com, Couponmom.com, and

CouponNetwork.com. I particularly like CouponMom.com since they have exact resources for your individual area, even matching sales to coupons at your favorite stores to shop. They also provide instructional videos to help explain how to use coupons to get free food. I really do recommend this resource to anyone just starting out.

You can also get coupons loaded to your store card. If you go to Kroger.com there is a coupon section. Just tick off the coupons you want and they are pre-loaded onto your Kroger card.

Walgreens also has quite a few opportunities to save with their balance rewards program, their register receipt program, and the rebates program that gives you 10% extra if you place your rebate on a Walgreens card. Walgreens also has a monthly savings circular that has great coupons in it.

Coupons can also be gotten by writing to the companies of the products you use most often. Once I wrote to a company about their new tuna fish cracker snack packs. I told them everything I liked and what I thought could be improved on. I got 5 coupons for a free snack pack.

The key to shopping with coupons is to get the smallest size the coupon will allow for at the lowest price. This may mean you have to collect hundreds of coupons in order to find a coupon for what you need. I personally get duplicates of them all.

Another important factor in couponing is the expiration date. I prefer coupons without expiration dates. These are rarer than blue diamonds to find. Most clipping services charge extra for them. It's important to go through your stash of coupons weekly and throwaway any that are expired. It is unethical to use a coupon after it expired, because that becomes stealing.

The real trick is to get coupons for the things that will be going on sale soon. Again, your price book is priceless in this task. Then to have a couple of them so you can stock up your pantry at this super low price. If you combine a sale price with a coupon, or better yet a coupon that is doubled or tripled, you can get food for next to nothing.

When I was a lot younger and living much leaner with four little girls, I managed to finagle the coupon jackpot. I had a purse full of carefully sorted and arranged coupons, a few rebates, and a store gift card that I bought for 95 dollars, but had 100 dollars of credit on it. With my husband and all of the children, I stalked the isles. I was so disappointed at first that I couldn't find anything. Then I came upon the "reduce/sale" bin. In each store, there is always the reduced bin or cart.

I found in this bin a bunch of canned goods that I had plenty of coupons for. I hurriedly grabbed everything that I had a coupon for. According to the sale prices written on top of the cans, I had about 70 dollars in goods. Then I proceeded to go around with my remaining 30 dollars and get fresh foods and meats.

When I reached the checkout, I asked the girl to ring each item in and then give me the sale price so that it would work out ok in the computer system. She did so happily. Then I handed over all of my coupons. She rang them all up. A few of the coupons rang up as double coupons. At the end, I paid less than the 30 dollars in stuff I got for full price. Had I bought no meat or fresh vegetables, my order would have been free. The clerk was astonished and asked her boss to come over. Sure enough, she rang it up correctly. All this created a small commotion. Plenty an elderly lady patted me on the back on the way out telling me "that's the way you do it."

Although I was capable of doing this once, it is hard to repeat. You have to be willing to forgo all personal preferences and just buy what you can for free or for pennies on the dollar. It just so happened that day that almost everything I needed was on sale and that I had a coupon for each thing. It's akin to the stars aligning. That doesn't mean you can't drastically reduce your food bill with coupons however. If you buy on sale, with a coupon, the smallest, cheapest, product that fits your coupon, you can get food for free or nearly so.

A favorite way I like to use coupons is for toothpaste, mouthwash, deodorant, and other personal care items at the dollar store. I will collect one-dollar manufacturer coupons for items I know are at the dollar store for a dollar. Then I will bring them in and pay for the items with coupons. This is a little easier than buying food. Since the price is a known, the product is known, and then it only becomes a search for the right coupon. It's the lazy way to get free food and personal items.

Another thing that acts like a coupon is competitor's sale papers. Collect up all the sale papers in a 20 to 30 mile radius. Then go to the one store that has the most products, at the lowest normal prices, and that honors the sale prices of its competitors. Use the sale papers to bring their prices down to everyone else's and then add coupons to the mix to bring the prices down even further.

Companies that will lower their prices are often sticklers for it being the exact same product, right down to the ounces advertised on the flyer. Also, don't argue if they refuse to honor another stores prices, just walk out and go to the next best retailer that does.

What do you do when a store advertises something but runs out? You go up to the customer service center and get a rain check. These are usually good for one month after they are written. It doesn't matter if they have one flavor of the item you wanted, if they are out of the other, go up and request a rain check. A rain check is like a coupon that extends the sale for you until the store can have the item in stock and you are shopping.

Kroger has sales about once a year where eggs are one-dollar a dozen. These eggs go fast, like in hours. I often came in with a free egg carton coupon for the dollar eggs, only to find they had sold out. I had to get a rain check numerous times in order to get the free eggs. When I get a rain check, I usually buy 10 or more of the item. We bought ten dozen eggs when I came back to shop and the boy at the counter thought it was weird, until I explained that one carton is one day of breakfast for my large family. He said I should get some chickens.

Finally, there is one more way you can reduce your food bill. About once a year, grocery stores will sell their own store card at a discount of 5 or 10 percent. The more money you can put down on that store card, the more money you can save later on. It's a good idea to save your money for this once a year discount.

Even if you normally purchase just 30 percent of your food at this one store, you can save a significant portion without chasing sales, or cutting coupons. If you happen to have a credit card that gives 5 percent cash back on purchases at grocery stores, you could purchase the discounted store gift card with that credit card and then pay the credit card off when you get home. Now you have saved 10 to 15 percent off the entire food bill before you've even shopped for sales, use competitor prices, used coupons, used rain checks, or looked in the sale cart.

Chapter Six: The Ultimate Shopping Trip

To have the ultimate shopping trip, you need everything prepared. The first thing is time. You should get up early, eat a good breakfast, and know that this is going to take the whole day. It's like going hunting, but without the smell of deer urine on your clothing.

The next thing you absolutely must have is your price book. This will make sure you have historically low rates for your area.

Have all of the local sale flyers ready to go. Make sure you have your coupons matched to the sales that each store is having. Make notes of the places that will honor a competitor's price. Circle the lowest prices of all the papers with a big red or black sharpie so the cashier isn't confused.

Have a grocery store gift card that was bought on discount with plenty of cash ready to go spend. So much the better if it was bought with a credit card that gives cash back for grocery purchases and you have already paid off the credit card. By doing this you have already saved money, before you even put it to work.

Match all your coupons to the flyers. This is where you would paper clip together your duplicate coupons that are going to be used for items on sale. These coupons you will use without a doubt. Once you go to the store, there may be things in the sale or discount bin in addition that you have coupons on also that you were unaware of before arriving.

Get all of your rain checks out and match them to your coupons. You may have to go to a few stores to get them all used. Just be certain you can use them and try to have a coupon for the items you plan to buy with them.

If you plan on going to more than one store, plan your route so that it is most efficient gas wise. Often I will go to Kroger, then ten blocks down to the day old bread store, then down the street to Walmart, then to the dollar tree, and on my way out of town towards home, I will stop at the gas station and pick up propane for 13 dollars for 20 pounds. By planning your route, you can make sure not use anymore gas than you need.

Make a mental note of which places match competitor's prices and offer double coupons. You should shop these places first. Make sure to have a copy, of each stores policy for coupons, rain checks, price matching, and gift cards. This helps to prevent any confusion on your or the cashiers part.

When you enter the store, make a beeline to the sale items advertised for which you have coupons already. These items tend to sell out fastest. Only buy as many as you have coupons to discount. Next, find the discount or sale cart and look through it very carefully. Try to match any products with coupons you may have. My general rule is that I will buy something without a coupon if, it is discounted 80 percent, I have a rebate slip which will make it almost free, or I have a small coupon for the item which will be doubled and bring the price to less than 80 percent of the original price.

Throughout this, you must check your price book, coupon carrier, and rebate slips. This is the most time consuming part of the whole trip. After you are satisfied that you have found the most items possible for the cheapest you can anywhere, it's time to move on to finding items that you have a rain check for.

Then after you have done this, go back over any of the sale items. Make a note of any that had a flavor sold out.

Check your loyalty card to see if you combine any purchases to reduce your food bill further. For example, if you picked up two discounted twelve-ounce cans of hunt's tomatoes and the store says that buying three will save you a dollar. Pick up the third one.

Take everything up to the checkout. For each item that will be reimbursed through a rebate, check them out separately according to how the rebate requires it, and get a separate receipt. Make sure the girl rings up all discounted items and then discounts them manually. Hand her any rain checks or coupons needed. Pay for it all with your gift card that you bought for a discount.

Before leaving, stop off at the customer service desk to collect any rain checks on items that were out of stock in the sale flyer that day, even if they were just a different flavor.

Then the real fun begins when you get home. Make sure you picked up plenty of Ziplocs.

Chapter Seven: Immediately After Shopping

Immediately after you get home from shopping you have a lot of work to do. Remember those Ziplocs I talked about earlier? They are integral to the next five to seven hours of your life. Depending on what you plan to eat, you will need to cook seven to thirty days of food at one time.

Before you shut the book in disgust, hear me out. It takes as much time to make eight quarts of soup as it does two. It takes just as much time for 70 cookies as 24. In fact, just as much time to cook 24 chicken breasts as 96. This is where you get to be frugal with your time. There is one catch; you have to spend a good portion of your afternoon cooking.

Just think though, for the next seven to thirty days, you will not need to do more than heat and eat for dinner every night. You can even do it for breakfast. The choice is yours.

Since I didn't give you exact food lists of what to buy, I will give you a list of things I buy. These may not be the cheapest things in your area. However, these things are generally very cheap. I will also tell you what

I do with each thing. I will start out with single item recipes. I will work my way up to recipes with two and three items. Please bear with me. This may be a bit boring if you know how to cook already.

Lentils: Take your large pot. Place ¼ a pound of lentils per quart. If you have an 8-quart pot, you will need 2 pounds of lentils. Fill to the top and boil until tender. Once tender, add salt and pepper to taste. Let the pot stand until lentils are cool. Fill 1-quart Ziploc bags with lentil soup and lay flat on a cookie sheet in your freezer until frozen. Each quart bag feeds four.

Pinto Beans: Very similar to lentils, except the night before soak the beans in your fridge. Then the next day either boil in your pot ¼ pounds to a quart. Also, you could just put ¼ pound to a quart in your crock pot. If you have a 4-quart crock-pot, you would put one pound in. These are really good when drained of the water, mashed in a sauce pan with a masher, and heated with American cheese. Prepare the pintos mashed with either cheese (for premade refried beans) or plain. Fill Ziploc quart bags and freeze the bags, as they lay flat on cookie sheets in your freezer. Each quart bag feeds four.

Chicken: Chicken breast should be diced, baked, and bagged. I would put all the breasts on a cookie sheet or three and bake them at once. They are finished once they are to 165 F or 74 C. I dice and bag my chicken separate so that I can add it to stuff as I cook. I really like chili, so precooked kidney beans, precooked chicken, some sauce, and spices make an awesome throw together dinner. Save the juice of all cooked chicken in its own bag for future soups.

Please do not precook chicken legs. I have not found a way to make them taste good. I do however; use the leftovers of whole chicken and chicken legs for soup and broth.

Turkey: There is nothing like roasting and cutting four or five turkeys in twenty-four hours. First, you would make sure the turkey is thaw. Sometimes they come from the store thaw. Other times, you have to thaw them out. Thaw them in the fridge on the lowest shelf, on a platter all their own. You can thaw in cold water if you change the water every 30 or so minutes. It takes less time than thawing in the refrigerator, but it is not a fast way. Expect 30 minutes per pound in a cold-water thaw or a day per 5 pounds in the refrigerator.

Preheat your oven to 325 F or 162 C. Place your Turkey (s) in. Let them cook 30 minutes for every pound. Baste them in their own juices to keep them moist. Poke them with a fork to allow the juice to sink into the turkey flesh. You don't need to season turkey. It is delicious on its own. Use a meat thermometer to know when your turkey is finished. It should read 165 F or 74 C in the center of each breast and each leg, without touching the bone.

Once your turkey(s) is done, carve it (them) carefully. Take all the white breast meat and place it in a bag or two. This can be used for hot turkey sandwiches, sliced turkey for the meat component of your dinner, or even cold cuts. Then fill a quart or two with dark meat. The dark meat is used for turkey and vegetable soup, turkey salad, pasta salad with turkey, and more. After all of the white and dark meat has been bagged and frozen, collect the drippings from the pan. This may require additional water. Place it over the stove and heat the pan with the water to release the drippings from the pan. Then place the water and drippings in a quart bag. This is great both for soups.

Once the carcass has been picked clean of all meat, break the bones, and boil them in a saucepan. This will release the marrow from inside and is very good for soups. Once the marrow has been released, pour the broth off into a bowl to cool. Then bag the broth for future turkey vegetable soup. This process of breaking down a turkey applies to all foul excluding geese.

Broccoli: Assuming you didn't buy pre-frozen broccoli, which you really should, you would take your steamer out, steam it lightly, place it in quart bags, lay the quart bags on cookie sheets, and freeze them lying flat on cookie sheets. I buy pre-frozen broccoli when possible.

Oatmeal: All oatmeal is put up in the proper bucket. All grains are stored in their dry bucket and cooked at the time of the meal. Oatmeal can be cooked, portioned out into family meal sized servings, and frozen ahead of time.

Rice: I do not pre-cook rice several days in advance. I may cook a double batch and put the rest in the fridge, but rice does not freeze well easily. That said, rice only takes about 20 minutes.

Eggs: Eggs do not need special treatment unless you intend to keep them for months. I buy five dozen eggs at a time for $8 and they are eaten by the end of the month. Eggs are very cheap protein that keeps a relatively long time fresh. At $2 a carton, you get on ounce of protein for 16 cents. That is exceptionally inexpensive in today's market. At $3 a carton, it's 25 cents for an ounce. Considering you only need 2 to 3 ounces at each meal, it is very cheap. That's equivalent to $2.56 per pound and $4 a pound respectively. Locally, I pay roughly 13 cents an ounce. That doesn't mean you can't find cheaper meats. You can, but you will have to hunt for it.

Peppers: Dice, steam for a minute (this is called blanching), place in bags, and freeze. I use sandwich bags for this. These are later used for Mexican rice, American fried rice, soups, chili, egg salad, and more.

Onions: Dice, blanch, bag into sandwich bags and freeze. These are later added to soups, pasta salads, turkey or chicken salad and egg salad.

Greens: This is meant for excessive greens. In general, we don't end up with many extras but when we do this is what I do. I dice the greens, blanch for one minute, bag, and freeze. Later they make healthy additions to soups. It doesn't matter if it is mustard greens, collards, kale, turnip greens, spinach, or orach. All of them can be used in soups and add a lot of vitamins to the soups. Every meal should have greens.

Celery: These are sliced, blanched for two minutes, bagged, and frozen. These are great for all sorts of salads, egg salad, potato salad, turkey salad, etc...

Spaghetti Sauce: I buy this for about a dollar a jar. Canning it is cheaper after the first year, if you grow your own tomatoes. Put it up in the pantry and use in chili, pasta, American Fried rice, Eggplant Parmesan, and several other tomato based dishes.

Root Crops: Such as carrots, turnips, rutabagas, etc... are placed in the fridge. I use them as snacks and as additions to soups and salads.

Potatoes: These are kept in the pantry either in sawdust, or in a bag. We use about 25 to 50 pounds of potatoes a month for a very large family. Most people could easily get by with 15 pounds. They can be used in almost everything. The skins are the most nutritious part of them.

Noodles: We store these in the pantry. We do not buy many noodles, as they are not very nutritious. These are for pasta and pasta salad.

Eggplant: Eggplant is always placed in the refrigerator and used within three days. Eggplant gets "seedy" quickly. This ruins the taste.

Summer Squash: These are diced when immature and blanched for two minutes. They are bagged. Then they are frozen for later use in pasta sauce, breads, cakes, and soups.

Winter Squash: We take the shell of off these with an ax, cube, blanch for a few minutes, bag, and freeze. We use these for soups, pies, breads, cookies, cakes, and more. It is hard to over blanch winter squash.

Cabbage: This is kept in the refrigerator. Sometimes it's turned into sauerkraut with some salt. Usually, I shred it and add it to soup to add some bulk. Cabbage soup is a fine light lunch. Just shred the cabbage thinly, boil some water, once it is to a rapid boil drop the shredded cabbage in and a bouillon cube. Stir once or twice and remove from heat before it is cooked through, but not before it has been heated through. Your cabbage should be stiff in spots yet, but warm all the way through. Stir in the flavor cube until dissolved, add pepper to taste, and enjoy. If you have no bouillon cube add salt, pepper, and a pat of butter. Cabbage soup does not freeze well. You cannot live on cabbage soup alone. This a light lunch for when you are in a rush, as it takes no time at all.

Spices: We buy spices dried and place them in the pantry, when we buy them. Common spices which are great to have around are, salt, pepper, chili powder, cayenne pepper, paprika, oregano, basil, parsley, garlic powder, thyme, rosemary, and sage. We like to have vanilla and cream of tartar too. These are stored in a dark cool place.

Cheese: Assuming you're not lactose intolerant, cheese is a favorite with most people. We freeze our cheese in the package we brought it home in. We do not buy pre-shredded cheese. If we plan to make 12 quarts of chili when we get home from shopping and freeze the rest, we will leave it unfrozen.

Chapter Eight: Recipes

Now that you know how to store individual items, you might want to get to cook your meals for the next 30 days. We will start with easy to store breakfast items, from there easy lunches, on to easy dinners.

Breakfast: The easiest breakfast is a piece of fruit and a glass of milk. This isn't enough for everyone though, and it isn't the most inexpensive breakfast.

Oatmeal- For every serving boil 1 cup of water. Once it has reached a rolling boil, add ½ cup of rolled oats for each serving. Stir. Add sugar or molasses to taste. Add raisins or banana slices for added flavor. Time till done: 15 minutes. This is not a cook ahead and freeze meal.

Eggs- Take a skillet and place it on the flame. Add a pat of butter. Remember, the more you conserve on your butter, the more money you save. Crack two eggs over a bowl and remove any shells. Once the skillet is good and hot with the butter sizzling, add the two eggs. When the whites are solid, flip to cook the yolk. Alternatively, after cracking the eggs and removing any shell, you could beat them with a fork. Then you could add any number of things like peppers, onions, mushrooms, tomatoes, green onions, cilantro, bacon pieces, cheese, and more. Maybe even add a little salsa, hot sauce, or Pico de Gallo on the side. Then cook them until firm. Time till done: 10 minutes. This is not a cook ahead and freeze meal. This recipe serves one.

Muffins- Preheat the oven to 350 degrees F or 180 degrees C. Add 2 cups of self-rising flour, 1 cup of milk, 1 beaten egg, ½ cup or honey or sugar, and ¼ cup of oil or melted butter to a bowl. Add any flavorings you like such as raisins, cranberries, mashed banana, applesauce, apple pieces, or blue berries. Cook for about 20 to 25 minutes. If you stick a butter knife in the top, it should come out dry and clean when done. This makes 12 muffins. This recipe serves 12. Once taken out of the oven and cooled, they can be bagged and frozen.

Molasses Bread- 3 cups flour, 3 cups oatmeal, 1-cup molasses, ½-cup sugar, 1 tsp. cloves, 1 tsp. baking soda, 1 Tbsp. nutmeg, 1 Tbsp. cinnamon, 4 tsp. baking powder, and 3 cups milk. Mix in a large bowl. Place in well-buttered loaf pans and bake at 350 F or 180 C for about an hour until a butter knife comes out clean from the middle. Makes a very dark sweet bread. Makes 3 small loaves which is enough breakfast for a family of four for a week. Great served with butter and a glass of cold milk for breakfast. Optional items to add, dice dates, raisins, figs, apple pieces, cranberries, and pumpkin.

Biscuits- Preheat the oven to 450 F or 280 C. Add 4 cups all-purpose flour, 2 Tablespoons baking powder, 2 cups milk, 1 cup melted butter, and 1 Tablespoon sugar to a large cooking bowl. At this stage, you may add shredded cheese, chives, sausage, bacon, onions, peppers, garlic powder, pepper, or leave plain. Do not over stir, just enough to be mixed. Grease muffin pans or a cookie sheets well with butter. Then take a tablespoon and drop the batter onto the pans. Recipe makes 24 biscuits. This recipe serves 24. May be frozen after cooled. If the biscuits are left plain, they may be eaten with jam or gravy.

Anyone of these breakfasts are fine on their own. Some can be frozen ahead and thawed the day before. Others must be made and eaten immediately. With a handful of good recipes, breakfast should never get boring. Notice too, all these recipes can be modified to add greater variation. I leave a few hints in each recipe how to do this.

Lunch: Lunch is a meal we skip, have to bring to where ever we work or go to school, or get on the go. It's always cheaper to bring lunch, unless you get it free. Some of these lunches will require a thermos.

Refrigerator Soup- Any soup will do but how do you make it? Take your large pot. I am going to assume it is 8 quarts. Put any scrap of vegetable from the refrigerator in it that is starting to go bad. In general this is how my soup goes, 4-6 potatoes, 3-5 carrots, 1-3 onions, ¼ a head of cabbage, a turnip, a green pepper, a handful of left over corn, some left over lima beans, a tomato, a handful of spinach on its last day, and some ginger grated into the pot. Then, I add a cup to a cup and a half of pre-cooked chicken or turkey. I let this simmer on my stove or in my crock-pot. As it cooks, I add a quart of the chicken broth. Then I add some garlic powder, salt, pepper, parsley, and a little basil. After 2-3 hours, depending on how small I cut all the vegetables, I have 8 quarts of nice soup. I take this after it has cooled and freeze it in small Ziplocs if it is for single servings or quart bags for the entire family. There are enough servings for a family of four to have lunch eight times. One quart is enough for a family of four. Measure out one cup for one serving. This is enough lunch for

32 days or it is 32 servings. This can be placed in quart bags and frozen. This can also be carried in a thermos and served with homemade bread.

Chili- Again, assuming an 8-quart pot, we will make some chili. Take out 4-quart bags of pre-cooked kidney beans. Also, take out a pound of ground meat. Fry up the pound of ground meat. At the same time, dump the 4-quarts of kidney beans into your large pot. Add 2 quarts of sauce, and place on low heat. Add chili powder to taste, garlic powder to taste, dice peppers from the freezer, diced onions from the freezer, shredded cheese as long as it isn't cheddar, tofu if you want, or anything else that would taste good in chili. If you want a really hot chili add some cayenne pepper. Add no more than ¼ tsp. per quart. When the meat is completely cooked, add it and the fat to the pot. Stir. Keep on medium to low heat until small bubble start to rise to the surface. Take it off the heat. This recipe makes 28 servings. Will feed a family of four 7 times. Each serving is a cup. This can be placed in quart bags and frozen. This can also be carried in a thermos and served with some crackers or homemade bread.

Lentil Soup- As previously stated, boil two pounds of lentil in an 8-quart pot for 2 hours. Add salt, pepper, butter, onion, garlic powder, shredded carrot or ham to taste. I sometimes even add tiny little pieces of potato, no bigger than an aspirin, in mine before I boil it. The choice is really yours. This makes 8-quarts of lentil soup, which is 32 servings or eight dinners for a family of four. This can be placed in quart bags and frozen. This can also be carried in a thermos and served with a slice of homemade bread.

Thin Potato Soup- This is called thin potato soup, because it is not the rich, buttery, delicious kind most people have become accustomed to. My mother made this when I was small. Peel eight to ten potatoes. You want to scrape the peel off here. Dice all the potatoes to about the same size. They should be the size of a penny. Add to the 8-quart pot. Then dice three onions and add to the large pot. Brown up a pound ground meat if you have it. While browning the meat, slice celery very thin. Used 1 head of celery for 8-quarts. Each slice of celery should be almost translucent. Add ¼ a stick of butter to the pot. Then add five to six quarts of water to the pot. Make sure there is at least three to four inches of clearance at the top. Add salt, pepper, parsley, and chives. Then add the pre-cooked ground meat. Place the pot on medium to high.

Cook until the potatoes are tender. This makes 32 single servings or 8 servings for a family of four. This can be placed in quart bags and frozen. One cup is equal to one serving. This can also be carried in a thermos and served with a slice of homemade bread.

Eggs Sandwich- One pan fried egg on bread. You break an egg over a hot buttered skillet and fry until firm. Then you add the egg to two pieces of bread. You could add caramelized onions to add flavor. This is not cooked ahead and frozen.

Potato Salad- 5-8 medium potatoes, 4-6 eggs, 1 Tablespoon of mustard, 1 tsp. of vinegar, 1/2 cup of mayonnaise or salad dressing, 1 large pickle (optional), 1 Tablespoon of dill (optional), 1 teaspoon paprika, and a dash of pepper.

Peel potatoes, dice to the size of a penny, and boil in your large pot. In your small saucepan hard-boil your eggs. *To hard boil eggs*, place the eggs in your saucepan and fill with water, then set over a flame. Once it reaches a rapid boil, count ten minutes. At the end of ten minutes, drain the eggs in a colander and run cold water over them. Take the shell off and discard it into the compost container. Put the eggs in a large bowl; add mustard, mayonnaise, diced pickle, dill paprika, and pepper. Cut the eggs into the mixture with two butter knives as if you were cutting lard into flour. If you are unfamiliar with this technique, mash it all with your masher until very few tiny egg white chunks are visible. This is your dressing for the potato salad.

After the potatoes are boiled until soft, drain them in the colander, and rinse with cold water to remove excessive starch. Add the potato salad dressing. If the potato salad is too dry, add more mayonnaise to taste. Optional things that may be added, chives, bacon bits, cracked black pepper, dice peppers, diced onions, shallots, etc...

Dinner: Dinner is usually the meal everyone sits down for at the table together. It is the final evening meal. It's time to catch up with the family, linger over parts of the day, and share with one another. It's an important meal, not just for the nourishment of our bodies, but also our minds.

Eggplant Parmesan- You will need 4-5 large eggplants, olive oil, spaghetti sauce, mozzarella cheese, parmesan cheese, ricotta cheese (optional), oregano, and rosemary.

First, slice your eggplant into strips. Then place your skillet over a flame, pour ¼ cup to ½ cup of olive oil into it, and slide strips of eggplant into the oil. Fry the strips in the oil until they are tender and the flesh pulls from the skin of the eggplant. You may need to add oil since eggplant soaks it up. You should use tongs to maneuver the pieces of eggplant and turn them gently.

When your first batch is finished, lay them gently in a large bowl that has a few layers of paper towels on the bottom. The paper towels help to soak up the excess oil. Continue with this process until the paper towels need changed.

Preheat your oven to 350 F or 180 C degrees. Then take your large pot and layer the bottom with strips of fried eggplant. Cover with a layer of sauce, then with a layer of ricotta cheese (Or mozzarella if you did not buy ricotta). Continue this process until you are out of eggplant. On the last cheese, add parmesan and mozzarella instead of ricotta. Sprinkle with oregano and rosemary. Place the pot in the oven and bake for 15 minutes. This can be frozen in quart bags. One quart is enough for a family of four to eat. This makes enough for about 8-quarts.

Chicken Stir Fry: Three cups pre-cooked diced chicken breasts, olive oil, 2 thin cut onions, 2-diced peppers, 2-Tablespoon chicken bouillon, 2 pounds or almost 1 kilogram frozen broccoli, and 1-cup rice.

First slice the pepper and onion thin enough they are nearly translucent. Then place your wok (only) on a flame and add a dash of olive oil. Fry the onion and pepper in the olive oil until caramelized. Then add the pre-cooked chicken, 1 cup of water, and cover to simmer.

Once your chicken has simmered well, add the 2 pounds of broccoli or roughly 1 kilogram of frozen broccoli. Replace the lid to cover it while it simmers. Once the broccoli is a nice bright green color and still quite firm, remove the lid to cook off any excess water.

Take your small saucepan and 1 cup of rice and two cups of water. Cover it with a lid and place it on the flame. Once it starts to boil over a little, reduce the flame to allow it to simmer. Keep the lid on until 20 minutes have passed after the boil stage. Once it has simmered for 20 minutes passed the boil, remove the lid and it should be perfect.

Lay a scoop of rice on the plate, with two scoops of the chicken broccoli mix over it. Then serve. Any excess chicken and broccoli mix can be bagged in quart bags and frozen. All excess rice should be placed in a covered dish in the refrigerator.

Chicken Dinner- This is a basic meat, veg, starch dinner. Preheat your oven to 350 F or 180 C. Take enough chicken legs for each person in the family to have one and thaw. Take enough potatoes for each person in the house to have one. Place thawed chicken legs on a cookie sheet. Place washed potatoes on another cookie sheet. Place both cookie sheets in the oven. Bake until the chicken in the center of each leg is no longer pink and a fork easily punctures the potatoes. (This usually takes an hour) When those are almost done, place some green beans in a saucepot and heat.

****Note** if you want to make lunch for tomorrow the same thing as dinner tonight, bake two of everything instead.

American Fried Rice- I use this meal with my left over rice from the nice before. Fry 1 pound of ground meat, 1-2 onions, 1-3 peppers, any greens around the house chopped finely about 3 cups, 1 12 ounce package of frozen corn and/or 1 quart of pre-frozen beans in the wok. Add oregano, basil, parsley, and garlic powder to taste. Fry until the meat is done and the onions are caramelized. Then add 1 quart of spaghetti sauce. Stir in well. After this is well mixed, add rice to fill out the wok. Take off heat immediately. Stir well. Add American or Mozzarella cheese as desired. You can also add eggplant, dice tomatoes, green chilies, chives, fresh garlic, spinach, turnip greens, mustard greens, and many other veggies to this dish.

Egg Dish- I'm not sure what this dish is called, but I discovered it when I had a lot of mouths to feed and little choices. This dish requires one well-buttered 9X9 baking pan. You can use a smaller one but I would not advise anything larger. First, you should have an overabundance of eggs, as this takes at least a dozen if not a dozen and a half. Second, you will need plenty of cheese, about 1 to 1.5 pounds. You will also need 2-3 cups of chopped greens, 1 can of hominy, and butter. Preheat the oven to 350 F or 180 C. Take the eggs and break them on by one in a small bowl. After examining to make sure no shell was allowed to enter the egg, dump the egg into a large bowl. Do this until 4 eggs have been broken. Scramble and place on the bottom of your baking well-buttered pan.

Place the pan with the eggs in the oven for about two minutes just to make the bottom slightly firm. Take the pan back out after the egg has barely set firm.

Then break the eggs one by one for the last 12 and add to a large bowl before scrambling. Add the hominy, greens, cheese, and also (optional) onions, mushroom pieces, bits of broccoli, small bits of cauliflower, diced bits of asparagus, or anything else on hand. Stir well. Add to the pan and place in the oven. Bake until a butter knife comes out clean and dry. The last minute before removing the egg dish, sprinkle cheese on top and melt. Remove from the oven. This dish serves 12. This is enough for a family of four to eat three times. It should be served with a fresh garden salad, and fruit.

Chapter Nine: Finding Food Free

Finding free food is like the holy grail of frugal eating. If you can get free food without asking for charity, you are extremely talented. However, very few people can attain this level of frugality.

First, let's explore some of the more extreme ways people find free food without asking for charity. The most extreme example is dumpster diving. There is actually a movement centered on dumpster diving called freeganism.

The premise here is to live on the scraps that our bloated and over consuming society throws away. I will admit I have dumpster dived in my youth. When I was a teenager, I readily boasted that I could survive off what most people tossed in the dumpster. It was a way of life for me as a kid.

There are downsides, like rotten food, maggots, dead animals, and more. Also, once you get older there is the concept of shame. That doesn't mean becoming a freegan is bad, it's just some people can't accept that dumpster diving is a perfectly acceptable way to get one's daily bread. The final issue though is legalities. In some states, garbage is "owned" by whoever throws it out until it is picked up by the trash company. It is always a good idea to ask permission if you see the owner, before diving in. You would be surprised how many people say go at it.

There are some rules for dumpster diving. First, don't tear up the trash. This disrespects the person you are foraging in the trash of. Second, take everything of value that can be recycled to save it from the landfill.

When I was younger, I found numerous trash bags full of new naked dolls. I didn't need forty naked dolls, but I took them anyway. Later, I made clothes for the dolls from other foraged items and donated the clean and dressed dolls to children in need for Christmas.

Some stores set aside the "good" garbage for foragers in nice clean containers. When I worked for a pizzeria in New Jersey, all the good "garbage" pizzas were placed in a clean pizza box on the top of the dumpster for the homeless people in the area. The "garbage" pizzas were simply pizzas that were never picked up before closing. There was nothing wrong with them at all.

I learned to dumpster dive from many people. My grandpa would pay me to dumpster dive for cans. When I was a homeless kid, a fellow homeless person taught me how to do it carefully and where the best places to find food were. It was often the only way I could make money to support myself. As a young adult, I taught upper middle class kids the art form, which they got a kick out of because it was taboo. In case you are wondering, grocery stores, fast food joints, and diners are the best places for food.

Dumpster diving carries real risks socially, physically, and legally. Socially it is a bit like having the plague unless your friends are open minded. Physically you can get hurt climbing into and out of dumpsters. Legally, you can be charged with theft if your state considers garbage owned by the owners until the trash company picks it up. I never suffered anything personally. Keep these things in mind before you commit to dumpster diving.

Another example of extreme ways to find free food is going to a store on the weekend just to eat the samples. This only works if most of your stores are in walking distance. Every Saturday Walmart has people that hand out samples of food. You can probably get a small snack if you eat at each station in the store. To be honest, it's like going to a wedding just to get a free dinner. Major faux pas but no one can prove anything. You will have to look at yourself in the mirror each morning though.

I consider this lower than dumpster diving. Why would I think such a thing? I consider dumpster diving "honest". Whereas this isn't remotely since you have no intention of every buying what they are advertising to you.

Another method of getting free food is to barter your time or services for it. This works several ways. You can offer to work in a friend's garden for a little surplus garden vegetables. You can offer to wash dishes in a restaurant in order to get a free meal. You can offer trade something you made or found dumpster diving for some food at the farmer's market.

Bartering is one of the oldest methods for humans to get what they need. It's often over looked as "inefficient" or "unnecessary", but in the alternative economy, everything is done through some sort of barter. You can get most of your consumable needs through bartering and dumpster diving alone.

The last way you can get free food, we have already discussed. You can use a dollar coupon to get food from the dollar store. This is easy to do, but the chances of having it happen often enough to keep you alive, is slim to none.

Of course there are many other ways to get free or cheap food such as; fishing, hunting, gardening, and foraging, but they all require skills which cannot even begin to be covered in this book. I do encourage you to learn these skills to enhance your ability to provide food for yourself from unlikely sources.